MANCHESTER IN 50 BUILDINGS

DEBORAH WOODMAN & PAUL RABBITTS

AMBERLEY

This book is dedicated to the memory of the late Samuel and Eric Kerfoot

First published 2019

Amberley Publishing, The Hill, Stroud
Gloucestershire GL5 4EP

www.amberley-books.com

British Library Cataloguing in Publication Data.
A catalogue record for this book is available from the British Library.

ISBN 978 1 4456 5922 0 (print)
ISBN 978 1 4456 5923 7 (ebook)

Typesetting by Aura Technology and Software Services, India.
Printed in Great Britain.

Contents

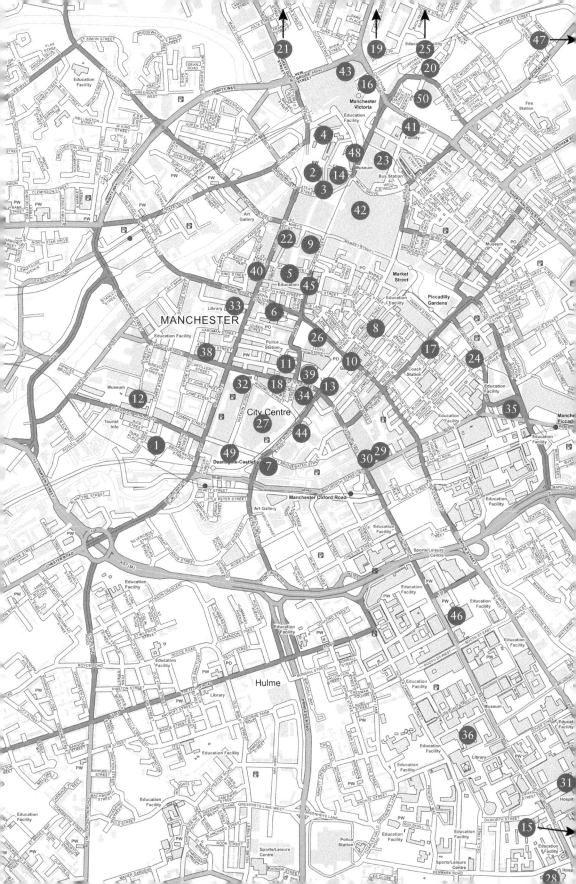

Key

Introduction

Manchester is a remarkable city. It boasts an eclectic mix of architecture that is reflective of its considerable past and it has been difficult to select just fifty buildings. Manchester is famous for the Industrial Revolution with its factories, working-class people and rapid urban development, all based around its production of cotton textiles, yet we see a diverse range of buildings that begins with Roman Mancunium, where a fort and civilian settlement existed from around AD 77 until around AD 400. Little is known about the intervening years but around AD 900 the Anglo-Saxons were known to have settled in the area around Manchester Cathedral and this became known as Mamecester. Albert Gresley, whose dynasty formed the Manor of Manchester, was successful in developing trade, and here we see the first glimpses of the textile trade for which Manchester became renowned. In 1301 Manchester was awarded a charter granting the townspeople privileges that effectively upturned the feudal system in the area. In 1309 the de la Warres inherited the barony and in the 1420s Thomas de la Warre created the Collegiate Church, which is now Manchester Cathedral.

Manchester grew and textiles became an increasingly important aspect of the local economy. Local merchant Humphrey Chetham used his wealth to create a Blue Coat school and after his death in 1653, his bequest was used to buy the surrounding buildings and a library was established. Chetham's Library is regarded as one of the oldest English-speaking public libraries in the world and is certainly the oldest public library in Britain. From around the 1750s inventions in textile production and changes in work practices from domestic textile production to a factory-based system led to what became the Industrial Revolution. This also led to a soaring population. In 1729, the first Cotton Exchange was built for trading. Other aspects of Manchester life were developing and this was reflected in its architecture, such as St Ann's Church in 1712, in response to differing religious beliefs that had emerged in the aftermath of the Civil War.

Manchester is most noted for its development during the nineteenth century. Industrialisation and urbanisation had created a hierarchy in a society comprising of a working class and a wealthy middle class. Politics could not keep pace with changes in a society where demands for a political voice were directed at a government mostly comprised of a landed gentry who did not want to part from their esteemed positions of power and status. Working-class discontent escalated into one of the most notorious episodes in Manchester's history. The Peterloo Massacre took place on 16 August 1819 when thousands gathered on St Peter's Field to hear radical speakers including orator Henry Hunt. Magistrates dispatched the Manchester Yeomanry Cavalry and an estimated eleven people died and several hundred were wounded, and it has left an indelible mark on the history of Manchester.

Manchester is renowned for its pioneering past. For example, in 1830 the first railway from Manchester to Liverpool ran, departing from Liverpool Road station, which is now the Science and Industry Museum. The first public library in Manchester opened in 1852 at Campfield. In 1847 the Collegiate Church became Manchester Cathedral and in 1853 city status was conferred. By 1851 the population of Manchester had reached 186,000 and immigration was a significant factor; for example during the late nineteenth century the population was boosted by the arrival of Jews fleeing persecution in Eastern Europe. The current town hall was built in 1877 to replace the limited space of the previous King Street location and was a symbol of civic pride. Manchester was a place of two halves and those doing well, did very well and for the middle class, life was very comfortable indeed. Manchester's middle class were keen to foster cultural institutions. These included the Athenaeum, the Portico and the Literary and Philosophical Society. The 'Royal Institution for the Promotion of Literature, Science and the Arts' was established in 1823 and a building to house the society began in 1829 and opened in 1834. It became Manchester Art Gallery in 1882. A number of middle-class men were Unitarians and attended Cross Street Chapel where William Gaskell (husband of novelist Elizabeth Gaskell) was a minister and here notable middle-class families were in the congregation and held civic office at one time or another.

Into the twentieth century, Manchester was badly damaged during the bombing campaigns in the Second World War. In fact, Manchester Cathedral was the second most bomb-damaged cathedral in the country after Coventry. However, a few of Manchester's iconic buildings such as the recently constructed Central Library and Midland Hotel escaped. Post-war, Manchester suffered economic decline that had begun during the interwar years. However, a revival began during the 1970s due to increased economic investment and the city witnessed a variety of regeneration schemes. The once Liverpool Road railway station became the Museum of Science and Industry in 1969. In the 1980s the Roman site at Castlefield became an urban heritage park including a reconstruction of the Roman fort. In 1984, the Jewish Museum opened. The G-Mex Centre opened in 1986, turning this former derelict goods yard into a concert and exhibition venue. The Bridgewater Hall, home to the Hallé Orchestra and the BBC Philharmonic, opened in 1996. The Arndale Centre, constructed in the 1970s, is one of the largest shopping centres in Europe, and while initially not regarded as a fine example of architecture, it remains a focal point of the city's retailing district. This, alongside surrounding buildings and streets, was badly damaged as a result of the IRA bombing of 1996. The subsequent revival of this area has transformed the city centre.

Manchester in the twenty-first century is a remarkable and flourishing cosmopolitan city. Older manufacturing industries have been largely replaced by thriving service industries. This success can be seen in many of the city's new buildings such as Beetham Tower, the tallest building in Manchester and constructed in 2006, and the new Co-operative building at No. 1 Angel Square as part of the NOMAD regeneration of the northern edge of the city.

The 50 Buildings

1. Roman North Gate, Castlefield

The origins of Manchester, or Mancunium, can be traced back to the Roman garrison that was constructed at Castlefield. It began as a wooden fort, built by the Roman army under the leadership of Gnaeus Julius Agricola on a high sandstone outcrop around AD 77. The fort was replaced with a stone garrison and the surrounding site underwent a number of modifications between around AD 160 and 200 as a civilian settlement grew around it to accommodate its increased size and military importance. The North Gate, whose reconstruction we see today, was located on a Roman road that ran from the military to the civilian settlement.

During the twentieth century a number of archaeological excavations took place, including work by Professor Barrie Jones of the University of Manchester's Archaeological Unit in the 1970s, and the Greater Manchester

The North Gate reconstruction, built in 1982. (© Ben Abel)

Original excavations carried out at the site. (© Ben Abel)

Archaeological Unit during the 1980s and early 2000s. This research has included a modern reconstruction of the impressive North Gate, built in 1982, and it is believed that by the middle of the second century the fort contained four of these gateways. The reconstructed North Gate contains an inscription that commemorates the detachment of Raetians and Noricans, who were groups of European soldiers stationed in Manchester, and Lucius Senecianius Martius, one of the only known Roman names associated with the area. Some of the finds include three buildings alongside the Roman road that ran from the North Gate, and they are thought to have been a shop, an inn and a house. The outer civilian area was known as the vicus and housed around 2,000 inhabitants. The garrison developed a range of trades to support the soldiers and their families, including blacksmiths and bakeries.

The fort at Castlefield was of strategic importance during the Roman occupation of Britain, at a crossroads between Chester and York, and north to Carlisle. However, in line with the decay of the Roman Empire, the site existed as a working fort until around AD 400, when the Roman army left Britain and it fell into ruin.

2. Manchester Cathedral

The current Manchester Cathedral is predominantly Victorian in construction, having undergone numerous modifications over many centuries. However, a church is believed to have been on the site since around AD 700, because a stone carving dating from Anglo-Saxon times known as the Angel Stone was found in the wall of the south porch. The cathedral's history is better recorded from 1421, when Thomas de la Warre, as its first rector, established the Collegiate Church and it is here that there are more detailed records about its development.

By the early 1400s it was decided that the number of parish priests was insufficient to cover Manchester's increasing ecclesiastical area, so Thomas petitioned both the pope and the monarch of the day, Henry V, to grant him a license to establish a Collegiate Church. The resulting college was dedicated to St Mary, St Denys and St George. Thomas bequeathed around £3,000 to finance the construction of the college buildings to house a number of priests, which began around 1422. Unfortunately, there were insufficient funds to complete the project properly and some of the buildings had to be completed in wood, and it has even been suggested that stone from the Roman site at Castlefield was used in the construction. Thomas died in 1426, before he had a chance to see his work completed. The college was dissolved in 1547 by Henry VIII's successor, Edward VI, who made several religious changes. However, this was upturned with the arrival of Mary I, and Elizabeth I continued the tradition.

The Collegiate Church was granted cathedral status in 1847. It underwent a major refurbishment in the 1880s. The cathedral has suffered bomb damage over the years, including during the Second World War, when in 1940 it was hit by a German bomb, destroying much of the north-east section and taking around twenty years to restore. It became the second most bomb-damaged cathedral after Coventry. It was also affected by the 1996 IRA bombing, which caused further damage to the building.

An early twentieth-century postcard of the west end of the cathedral.

Above: A wonderful panoramic
view of the cathedral in
the Manchester sunshine.
(© Andrew Love)

Right: The stunning tower of
the cathedral. (© Ben Abel)

The majestic interior of the cathedral. (© Steven Heywood)

3. The Old Wellington Inn

The old Wellington Inn is believed to have been constructed around 1552 in a small street off Market Street known as the Shambles. Downstairs eventually became a public house but throughout much of its early life it contained a separate business on the upper floors, including a draper's shop, an opticians, and 'Ye Olde Fishing Tackle Shoppe'. During the seventeenth century it was the home of the Byrom family, where the notable writer John Byrom was born in 1692. It was originally two storeys high but during the seventeenth century an additional floor was added. Into the nineteenth century it became the Vintner's Arms and subsequently Kenyon Vaults but by the mid-1860s it was back to its original name of the Wellington Inn.

More recently the Old Wellington Inn has faced some major challenges. Like nearby Manchester Cathedral, it suffered bomb damage both in 1940 and 1996. During the 1970s, a time when the preservation of heritage was not a key priority, the inn was affected by the construction of the Arndale Centre, where it was raised on a concrete platform to fit in with the wider redevelopment. After the

IRA bombing of 1996, the Wellington Inn was systematically taken apart and relocated in the newly formed Shambles Square, reopening in 1999.

Today, the Wellington Inn adjoins Sinclair's Oyster Bar in Shambles Square and both remain in business. Sinclair's Oyster Bar is noted for its pub signage depicting John Shaw and his assistant Molly Maid. During the eighteenth century John Shaw owned a Punch House in the Shambles where many local merchants met after a day's trading, to consume the infamous punch drink. Shaw died in 1796, but the club which bore his name lasted until 1938, and it moved from pub to pub during its life. Molly Maid was infamous for removing customers who outstayed their welcome with her mop and bucket. There is a plaque commemorating John Shaw on the outside wall of nearby St Ann's Church, where he and his family are interred.

The Old Wellington Inn with the adjacent Sinclair's Oyster Bar. (© Ben Abel)

4. Chetham's Library

Chetham's Library is a jewel in central Manchester. It is the former manor house, constructed next to the cathedral in 1421. It was acquired through a bequest made by a local businessman, Humphrey Chetham, who was a successful cloth merchant and spent much of his acquired wealth purchasing land and pursuing philanthropic causes. During the latter stages of his life he contributed to the education of boys in Manchester who were suffering hardship and had no other means to enjoy an education, but whose parents were honest and industrious people. He died, aged seventy-two, in 1653 and was buried at the Collegiate Church, just a few yards from the Chetham's complex. His bequest led to the opening of Chetham's Hospital, which was, in fact, a Blue Coat school and hospital for local boys (it was regarded as a hospital due to its caring environment) and a distinctive library. The library began making acquisitions around 1655 and over the years it has amassed one of the rarest collections of books in the world.

During the 1840s, Chetham's Library became a meeting place for the political thinker Karl Marx and fellow Marxist Friedrich Engels. Engels was no stranger to Manchester since his family established a factory in nearby Weaste, known as Erman and Engels. Engels' radical political thinking and observations of Manchester life resulted in the publication of the *Conditions of the Working Class in England* in 1845. Their visits to Chetham's Library are believed to have underpinned their Marxist ideology with the publication of their highly influential *Communist Manifesto*.

Entrance to Chetham's Library.

Above: Chetham's Baronial Hall. (© Mike Peel)

Below: The interior of Chetham's Library. (© Michael D. Beckwith)

Today, Chetham's Library is the oldest public library in the English-speaking world and is one of the oldest surviving buildings in the Manchester region. It houses some very rare and old collections as well some more recent archives, such as that of Belle Vue, one of the major leisure attractions of the region in the nineteenth and twentieth centuries. It became a Grade I listed building in 1952. Chetham's School of Music exists on the same site, and the area is an eclectic mix of the old original manorial buildings and more modern constructions.

5. St Ann's Church

This iconic church, located in St Ann's Square, has both beauty and religious significance. During the eighteenth century, politics and religion became complicated following the Civil War of the 1640s and subsequent restoration of the monarchy. The Collegiate Church had become associated with the Tory Party and the 'high church'. However, it was felt that there a need for a place of worship that followed a Whig tradition, who supported the 'low church'. The 'low church' in Manchester had been represented by Dissenters (who had separated from the Church of England) and who worshipped at Cross Street Chapel. Its preacher, Henry Newcome, died in 1695 and Lady Ann Bland, daughter of the lord of the

A late Victorian scene in St Ann's Square dominated by the church.

St. Ann's Square   Manchester

Hunt's Series M/c.

manor, Sir Edward Mosley, embarked on a mission to provide an alternative means of worship. In 1708 an Act was passed to build St Ann's Church. The foundation stone was laid by Lady Ann in 1709 and the church was consecrated by the Bishop of Chester, Sir William Dawes, in July 1712. It became surrounded by the fashionable St Ann's Square and this was an attempt to remove the focal point away from the Collegiate Church.

St Ann's has a neoclassical design that is believed to be the work of John Barker. It was originally constructed of local sandstone, which has been partially replaced over successive restorations. In 1777 parts of the original tower became dangerous and was replaced with a spire, but soon after this was again replaced with a new tower. It was originally fitted with plain glass, but more ornate stained glass was fitted during the nineteenth century. During the 1880s the interior was redesigned by the notable architect Alfred Waterhouse, who also designed Manchester Town Hall.

In recent times, St Ann's narrowly avoided serious damage during Second World air raids during 1940 and still houses a burnt-out incendiary bomb that fell on the roof. It also suffered moderate damage during the IRA bomb of 1996. Today, this Grade I listed building remains a jewel at the heart of the city centre.

St Ann's Church today, after a number of alterations and restorations over many years. (© James Hall)

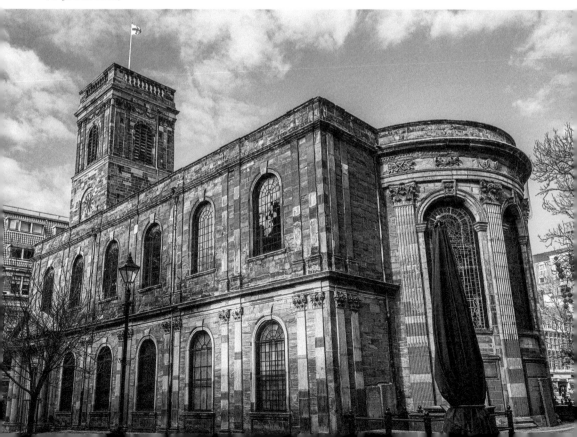

St Ann's Church with a statue of Richard Cobden in front. (© Ben Abel)

6. St Mary's Catholic Church

This striking Catholic church is often referred to as a 'Hidden Gem' due to its tucked-away location on Mulberry Street and impressive ornate architecture. The current building dates from 1848 but there has been a church on the same site since 1794. The Catholic priest Father Broomhead purchased land in Mulberry Street for the construction of the original church, which was financed by subscriptions that were raised, in some respects surprisingly, from people across a number of different faiths. Modern Mulberry Street is in the heart of affluent Manchester city centre, but during the eighteenth and nineteenth centuries it was particularly deprived, with poor housing and living conditions. St Mary's was specifically located to provide religious and moral guidance to a troubled and poverty-stricken community. During the earlier part of the nineteenth century, St Mary's underwent a series of renovations, including repairs to a collapsed roof in 1835. A cemetery was eventually incorporated into the vaults.

Between 1821 and 1837, Reverend Henry Gillow was the minister. He proved to be a particularly energetic priest, becoming chairman of the Catholic School Committee. He also took control of the St Mary's Mission. By 1848 a new church was constructed on the same site and its design was very different to other buildings in Manchester, where externally it looks like architecture that is more reminiscent of the Rhineland in Germany, and yet inside it has more of a Roman feel with its columns and ornate features. A Mr Lane of Preston did much of the interior, including a version of Da Vinci's *Last Supper* in stone and a statue of the Virgin Mary. By 1869 Father John Newton was the minister and during his tenure at St Mary's he employed the services of a sculptor to decorate the interior of the church. By 1872, Bishop Herbert Vaughan had arrived and during his time he founded the notable St Bede's College. He is also known to be the person who coined the phrase 'Hidden Gem' to describe the church, which has remained ever since. It became a Grade II listed building in 1963.

St Mary's Catholic Church, Manchester's 'Hidden Gem'.

7. Briton's Protection Public House

This unique hostelry is one of Manchester's oldest surviving public houses, and evidence suggests it was built around 1806. Its name reflects its original use as a recruiting centre for locals wishing to join up for military service during the Napoleonic Wars in the early part of the nineteenth century. Its interior is mainly based on 1930s architecture following refurbishment, and both its internal features and external inn sign depict scenes from the Peterloo Massacre in 1819, which took place just yards away in St Peter's Field.

Today, the Briton's Protection is a Grade II listed building close to the Bridgewater Hall and it is noted for its popularity with theatregoers and musicians. It is famous for its extensive whisky collection where it is reported to have over 200 varieties to choose from. The pub was voted 'Best Pub in Manchester' in the Pride of Manchester Awards in both 2008–09 and 2009–10 and remains an important tourist hotspot in the city.

The Briton's Protection public house, an iconic pub in the heart of Manchester. (© Mike Hedgethorne)

8. Portico Library

The Portico Library, founded in 1806, was an independent subscription reading room and library, designed for leading Mancunian merchants and gentlemen, who had witnessed the opening of the Liverpool Athenaeum and wished to see a similar facility in Manchester. Two businessmen in particular, Robert Robinson and Michael Ward, embarked upon its creation, paid for by subscriptions at a cost of nearly £7,000. It comprised a newsroom, which during the early nineteenth century was one of the only places where London newspapers could be accessed, a library and a reading room. Its membership was a who's who of Manchester society, including the notable scientist John Dalton, politicians Richard Cobden and John Bright, and police force founder Sir Robert Peel. For many years its chairman was Reverend William Gaskell, husband of novelist Elizabeth Gaskell. At the outset, its membership was confined to affluent men, until after 1870 when women who qualified under the Married Women's Property Act could become members, and this allowed membership for notable women like Elizabeth Gaskell. However, before she could formally join the library, it is believed that her husband, William, borrowed books for her. Today, her novels are some of the most noted works in their collections.

The main entrance to the Portico Library on Mosley Street. (© Gary Bond)

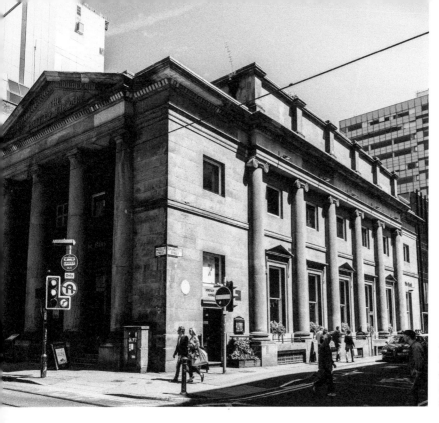

An impressive façade looking down Charlotte Street. (© Derek Stuart-Cole)

The building was designed by Thomas Harrison, an architect who had developed a reputation for producing great classical buildings in a Greek revival style, and the Portico was one of the first of its kind in the country, with an impressively ornate ceiling dome and four external ionic pillars and frieze. The original club was on two floors, but during the 1920s it faced financial difficulties and the ground level was leased to other businesses. The Bank of Athens was there for a while, but in recent times it has been a public house. The library contains an estimated 25,000 books, many of which were published in the nineteenth century and often first editions. It also has its own unique book classification system, which predates the Dewey Decimal System we are familiar with today.

9. The Royal Exchange

The Manchester (Royal) Exchange is one of the most impressive buildings in central Manchester. It currently houses the Royal Exchange Theatre Company but was originally a trading centre until it closed for business in 1968. It was once regarded as 'the largest room in the world', servicing the cotton industry that Manchester had become so famous for. Manchester's first exchange was built in 1729 but closed toward the end of the eighteenth century. However, it was quickly realised that a new building was required. This was opened in 1809 and was expanded over time. The current exchange building is the third exchange, constructed between 1867 and 1874. Again, this underwent further expansion during the interwar period. The Great Hall was the epicentre of cotton trading and this continued until 1968 despite being faced with the demise of the cotton trade after the First World War and struck by bombing during the Second World War. In fact, the last day's trading figures can still be seen on the large display board.

The Cotton Exchange, once the visible representation of Manchester's role in world trade, faced an uncertain future until a theatre company decided to test it for performances in 1973. This was a promising start to a totally new concept in theatrical entertainment and the Royal Exchange Theatre Company was officially formed in 1976.Ever since the theatre has put on many performances of Shakespeare and other classical works and it attracts some of our finest actors. It is a unique theatre experience where the theatre and seating are in a capsule in the centre of the Great Hall and performances are experienced 'in the round' giving the audience a sense of being part of the performance. It was unfortunate in facing damage for the second time due to the IRA bombing of 1996, but after two years of renovation the building opened once more.

The Royal Exchange in late Victorian times.

Much altered over the years, the Royal Exchange is still one of the most impressive buildings in Manchester. (© Ben Ponsford)

10. Manchester Art Gallery

Manchester Art Gallery occupies the building that began its life as the Royal Institution, a middle-class intellectual organisation that dates from 1823, where merchants and artists felt that there was a need for more cultural pursuits in a place that was more associated with industry. The Royal Institution was constructed between 1824 and 1835 in a Greek Ionic design by notable architect Sir Charles Barry, in a style that complements the neighbouring Portico Library. When its galleries opened to the public in the mid-1830s, it was technically open to everyone, but in reality a one shilling barrier existed for many working-class people who could ill afford the entrance fee. It was well supported by the middle and upper classes, which included the Duke of Wellington as one of its patrons. The Royal Institution was instrumental in supporting the Art Treasures exhibition held near Old Trafford in 1857.

One of its first acquisitions was *A Moor* by James Northcote. In 1882 it officially became the city's art gallery and transferred its daily management to Manchester Corporation, who agreed to provide around £2,000 each year for the following twenty years to purchase artwork. In 1913 some of the artworks were attacked by a small number of suffragettes who were campaigning for women's

The main entrance to the art gallery as designed by architect Sir Charles Barry. (© Ben Abel)

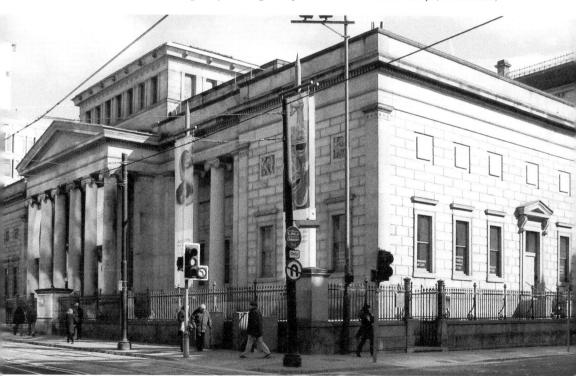

Manchester Art Gallery, home of some of the finest artworks in the country.

right to vote at the time. Lilian Williamson was imprisoned for three months and Evelyn Manesta for one month for the damage they caused.

The gallery has collected around 6,000 pictures, 250 sculptures and several thousand other artefacts, and is particularly noted for its collection of works by nineteenth-century artists, such as the Pre-Raphaelites including, for example, Dante Rossetti. Other works include art from some particularly notable artists of their generations, including Hogarth, Renoir, local artist L. S. Lowry, well known for his depictions of Manchester and Salford's working-class life, and his former tutor Adolphe Valette, who was also renowned for his early twentieth-century Manchester scenes. The Athenaeum, located at the back of the art gallery on Princess Street, also forms part of the modern gallery complex.

11. Friends Meeting House

The current Quaker's Friends Meeting House dates from 1828, but the original building on this site was constructed in 1795 since their original building on Deansgate had become too small for the growing congregation. The Quakers had been present in Manchester from around the mid-seventeenth century and it is known that they began work on their first meeting house in 1673 on Deansgate. Their work has always focussed on social causes and volunteering that has

Friends Meeting House, still a refuge for many to this day.

remained a constant thread from these early times to the present day. The original building was known to have offered refuge to some of those caught up in the Peterloo Massacre in August 1819. A Quaker's school was built in 1819 nearby at the corner of Mount Street, which proved significant in providing adult education.

By the 1820s the meeting house had become too small for the rapidly growing congregation and the present building was constructed on the same site. It was designed by architect Richard Lane in a neoclassical style, which was popular during the early nineteenth century, and the £7,600 building costs were raised by subscriptions from the local Quaker community. Members of the congregation at the Friends Meeting House became notable figures in Manchester's public life, and meetings were held that debated key issues of the day; for example, supporting the anti-slavery campaign and prison reform. Members included the scientist John Dalton, and founder of the *Manchester Guardian* John Taylor.

Into the twentieth century, the building underwent various renovations between 1923 and 1999, and more recently in 2012. Today, it provides a modern conference space in a historic setting. It continues its emphasis on social and economic justice where, for example, the building provides shelter in the winter to asylum seekers, and members continue to support a range of causes relating to equality and diversity, health, and poverty.

12. Science and Industry Museum

Manchester's Science and Industry Museum is devoted to the history of science and engineering and has a range of extraordinary machines that took us through the Industrial Revolution and beyond. However, the building itself has an even richer past as the former Liverpool Road train station that on 15 September 1830 saw the departure of the first railway journey between Manchester and Liverpool and is consequently the oldest passenger railway station in the world. Its significance is unparalleled in heralding the arrival of a whole new way of life for the passage of goods and people, joining Manchester with an efficient connection to the Port of Liverpool, transporting not only passengers but coal, cotton, foodstuffs and more.

Liverpool Road station closed to passengers in 1844 as other stations, such as Victoria and London Road (now Piccadilly), opened and it concentrated on the movement of goods thereafter. The modern museum comprises a series of original station buildings that includes the impressive ticket hall and the first railway warehouse. The new warehouse building came into operation in 1880, which included tracks running into the building to allow goods to be processed indoors. The Air and Space Hall originally opened in 1882 at Lower Campfield Market, selling produce twice weekly.

In 1969 the first North West Museum of Science and Industry was opened on Grosvenor Street, but this quickly outgrew its location. The Liverpool Road site, abandoned in 1971, was taken by the local Granada Television Studios, who used part of it for its Granada Studios tour and occasional filming of scenes from *Coronation Street*. In 1983 the museum was relocated to Liverpool Road for the first stages of the newly created Museum of Science and Industry. It opened on 15 September that year to coincide with the 153rd anniversary of the first rail journey.

Exhibits at the modern Science and Industry Museum are not confined to the railways, but also includes steam engines, textiles machinery and aviation. This includes a replica of 'Baby', the first programmable computer, which was developed in the city in 1948.

Above: The Air and Space Hall originally opened in 1882 as Lower Campfield Market.

Below: The former Liverpool Road Station Complex. (© Andrew Anderson)

Above: The former ticket hall and main station building. (© Ben Abel)

Below: The impressive entrance to the Air and Space Hall. (© Ben Abel)

13. Athenaeum

The Athenaeum currently forms part of Manchester Art Gallery. It began as the Manchester Athenaeum for the 'Advancement and Diffusion of Knowledge', forming part of a wider culture of education and leisure for middle-class merchants and intellectuals. In particular, the Athenaeum attracted a younger male middle-class membership. The concept behind the Athenaeum came from a local surgeon, John Walker, who, having entered into conversation with a group of young middle-class men that included the aspiring politician Richard Cobden, organised a meeting in 1835 to provide a facility designed for 'intellectual cultivation' with reading and newsrooms, a library, coffee room, and a regular lecture series.

They were originally housed in the nearby Royal Institution building, but by 1839 it was felt that they needed their own premises. Within weeks of inviting subscriptions over £10,000 was raised and this allowed the Athenaeum's construction on Princess Street, designed by Sir Charles Barry in an Italian palazzo style. There were around 1,000 subscribers who enjoyed the many events that took place, including the likes of Charles Dickens and Benjamin Disraeli. However, despite support from some of the most well known in local society,

The Athenaeum with its extra storey added in 1874. (© Max Hanna)

The Athenaeum, now joined to the adjacent art gallery. (© Rob Barnard)

the 1840s proved to be a particularly tough financial time for the Athenaeum and the club almost ended before it had truly begun. Thankfully, it overcame these difficulties and did indeed survive, and its membership grew to around 1,400. Its facilities included a 6,000-volume library, and members could study languages, enjoy musical events, poetry readings and recitals from notable writers. Richard Cobden, a key politician of his age who became the centre of Manchester's Liberal intellectual thinking and was pivotal in the Anti-Corn Law League, was a particularly noted member of the club.

In 1874 a fire destroyed the interior of the building and the restoration included a new lecture hall provided by adding an extra storey. The society lasted for around a century, closing in 1938, and here Manchester Corporation took charge of the building. In 2002 it became part of Manchester Art Gallery and as part of refurbishment both buildings were joined.

14. The Corn Exchange

The first Corn and Produce Exchange was opened in 1837 as a place for merchants to trade their foodstuffs. Prior to 1837 merchants used to congregate in nearby Hanging Ditch, and trading commenced each day with the ringing of a bell outside the Dog & Partridge public house in nearby Fennel Street. However, it became clear that a building specialising in foodstuffs was required. It was designed by Richard Lane at a cost of around £3,000. During the 1840s, the Corn Exchange became a key meeting place for the Anti-Corn Law League (ACLL). The ACLL was a group of Manchester manufacturers opposed to the Corn Laws, which was legislation that taxed imported grain and designed to keep prices high for cereal producers in Great Britain. However, the policy was disastrous, leading to starvation for many as food prices were too high. The ACLL was founded in 1838 by the local manufacturer and Liberal statesman Richard Cobden and Rochdale-born John Bright, who ran a campaign to reduce the tax on corn and oats to make food more affordable for working people. Their campaign was instrumental in the repeal of the Corn Laws in 1846.

The original building was replaced with a new construction between 1897 and 1903, which included an ornate interior glass dome ceiling. The depression of the interwar years had a negative impact on the Corn Exchange and by the end of the Second World War it faced an uncertain future. It became a place for small stall holders selling second-hand goods, records, clothing and jewellery, but in 1996 its fortunes were thrown into further chaos by the IRA bombing, which severely damaged the building and blew the glass dome ceiling apart. However, it provided an opportunity to consider new uses for the building as part of the wider redevelopment of the bomb-damaged area. It was refurbished and reopened in 1998 as the Triangle shopping centre, housing designer retail outlets. Recently, the building has undergone further redevelopment and includes restaurants and a hotel.

The Corn Exchange, significantly damaged in 1996 by the IRA bombing. (© Ben Ponsford)

Right: The Corn Exchange, transformed into a high-end shopping centre in 1998. (© Ben Abel)

Below: The interior of the Corn Exchange today – a far cry from its origins as a 'Corn and Produce' Exchange. (© Stephen Cahill)

15. Elizabeth Gaskell's House, No. 84 Plymouth Grove

This is the former home of the famous Victorian novelist Elizabeth Gaskell and her minister husband, William, who was the Unitarian minister at Cross Street Chapel. The house itself, a Grade II listed villa, was inhabited by the Gaskell family from 1850 until 1913 when their daughter Margaret died. It was a typical middle-class house of its time, located in one of Manchester's emerging suburbs and showcasing the family's affluence and social status.

As a middle-class woman, Elizabeth was expected to stay at home and care for her family, but she had greater ambitions than a purely domestic role. She supported a range of charities, particularly ones that aided the poor and children. In fact, she was concerned about living in such a fine house when she witnessed so much poverty in the region. The Gaskells were very much connected with the cultural and intellectual life of middle-class Manchester, mainly through William's prominence in the Literary and Philosophical Society and the Athenaeum, though Elizabeth did eventually gain membership of the Portico Library in her own right. Elizabeth channelled her observations in her novels. One of her key works about the struggles of Manchester working-class life was that of *Mary Barton*, published in 1848 just before they moved into Plymouth Grove. Other novels included *Cranford*, *North and South* and *Wives and Daughters*. Elizabeth was very much connected to the literary talents of the day and boasted of friendships of other notable literary specialists of their age including Charles Dickens, the Bröntes, John Ruskin and Thomas Carlyle. In fact, Charlotte Brönte and Charles Dickens were known to have visited the house on a number of occasions during the 1850s. Musical conductor Charles Hallé was also a regular visitor to the house. Elizabeth lived there until her death in 1865.

Author Elizabeth Gaskell's House.

The Gaskell House was Grade II listed in 1952, though this did not stop it falling into decay until 2009 when the Manchester Historic Buildings Trust began its renovation. It was open to the public in 2014, having been restored to its original style and opulence.

16. Victoria Railway Station

Victoria railway station is one of three mainline stations that service central Manchester, alongside Piccadilly and Oxford Road. Victoria station is worth particular mention because of its original Victorian features. It was opened in 1844 and housed just one platform. The success of the railways ensured it was expanded over successive years, and by 1909 it contained seventeen platforms, and at one time had the accolade of housing the longest platform in Europe.

The Beeching Report of 1963 had a detrimental effect on Victoria, like many rail stations, and the number of platforms was reduced to deal with declining demand, which continued until around 1992 when it went through a major renovation and redesign and became attached to the new Manchester Arena. It suffered damage in 1996 from the IRA bomb, mainly due to glass blowing out. In 2009 it was

Victoria railway station, which retains much of its Victorian features. (© Ben Abel)

Above: The ornate ironwork to the exterior of this fine Victorian building. (© Ben Abel)

Below: Modernisation of Victoria station has continued as part of required improvements to its facilities. (© Ben Abel)

voted the worst station in the United Kingdom due to its poor facilities and this prompted further refurbishments, including a major roofing project. This project has allowed the station to retain some of its fine Victorian architecture and design, such as its exterior canopy and ornate Victorian tiling and mahogany wood finish.

17. Britannia Hotel

Today, the Britannia Hotel is a popular place for tourists, though it has a Victorian opulence that disguises the fact that it was originally built as Watt's warehouse, which traded in drapery and textiles. Watt's warehouse was built during the 1850s in an Italian palazzo style, and at six storeys became the largest and most opulent of its kind and the largest single-occupancy warehouse, since many buildings of this nature often contained multiple businesses. It took around seven years to plan the building and a further two to construct. It was owned by James Watts and his nephew Samuel. James was a former mayor of Manchester and local entrepreneur who started a small cottage business in nearby Didsbury and grew to become an important industrialist who made important political and business connections. He resided at Abney Hall in Cheadle and such was James' influence, Prince Albert chose to stay with him when he visited Manchester to attend the Art Treasures Exhibition of 1857. The building cost around £100,000 to construct and was planned to showcase Manchester's role in world trade, with dimensions of 300 feet long, 100 feet high and containing four prominent roof towers, its design offering space and light where goods could be inspected prior to purchase.

The Britannia Hotel, a former warehouse designed in an Italian Palazzo style.

The Britannia Hotel, originally a building planned to showcase success, affluence and Manchester's role in world trade.

Watt's warehouse suffered the loss of a number of its employees in the First World War, and this is commemorated by a sculpture erected in 1922 in the main entrance. It was also hit by German bombing during the Second World War but managed to survive. As the textiles industries declined in the region during the twentieth century, it left buildings like Watt's warehouse derelict and facing demolition. However, this landmark was saved from such a fate and in the 1980s it was remodelled and the Britannia Hotel was opened in 1982. Its Victorian interior remains the cornerstone of the hotel's interior including a particularly grand staircase and chandeliers.

18. Free Trade Hall – Radisson Edwardian Hotel

The former Free Trade Hall has become a hotel in recent times, but it played a fascinating and important part in Manchester's political and cultural life. A red plaque on the exterior commemorates the Peterloo Massacre in 1819 since the Free Trade Hall stands on St Peter's Field where this took place. It was constructed in the 1850s in recognition of the passing of the Corn Laws in 1846 and was symbolic of Manchester's Liberal political tradition of the nineteenth century, where politicians such as Richard Cobden and John Bright promoted free trade. Richard Cobden donated a piece of land at St Peter's Field and a temporary structure was erected in 1840. The Free Trade Hall seen today is the third structure on the site and was commissioned through public subscription. It was completed in 1856 as a public hall, and by 1858 it had become the home of Charles Hallé's famous orchestra, remaining their home until 1996 when they relocated to the newly built Bridgewater Hall.

The hall was prominent in local political life. For example, in 1905 suffragettes Christabel Pankhurst and Annie Kenney attained wide publicity for their campaign when they interrupted a meeting of the Liberal Party at the Free Trade Hall. Christabel questioned Winston Churchill, who was speaking at the event – if the Liberals were elected would they give women the vote? After repeating the question and demanding an answer, which they were never likely to receive, they were ejected from the meeting and finally arrested when Christabel spat at a policeman.

The Free Trade Hall also had a moment in cultural history when one of the most iconic concerts took place at the Lesser Free Trade Hall by the Sex Pistols in June 1976, and despite only around forty actually being there many more declared 'I Was There', such was the cultural influence of the event, sparking musical talents that went into the 1990s and 2000s in Manchester's vibrant music scene.

Above left: The Free Trade Hall, constructed in the 1850s.

Above right: The Free Trade Hall, the scene of political meetings and for many decades 'punk rock' mayhem.

The Free Trade
Hall, now
a high-class
Radisson hotel.

19. Joseph Holt's Brewery

Joseph Holt is named after its nineteenth-century founder and is a rare example of a brewery remaining in the same family hands in an industry dominated by larger companies and takeovers. The brewery still manages around 128 public houses in north-west England and supply beer nationally.

Joseph Holt was born in 1813 near Bury, and initially he worked at the Strangeways Brewery (that became famous for Boddingtons beer) during the 1840s. In 1849 Joseph set up his own brewery in Manchester and by 1855 he had taken over the Ducie Bridge Brewery on Cheetham Hill Road. By 1860 he had purchased a piece of land to build the Derby Brewery on Empire Street in Cheetham Hill and here he also built the family home.

In 1882 Joseph handed over the brewery to his son Edward, so when Joseph died in the family home at the Derby Brewery in 1886 the transition in management was seamless. By this time he had grown the business to include around twenty tied houses around the region. The 1880s was a time for the prolific purchase of public houses and Edward continued to acquire many properties. During the 1890s the brewery underwent modernisation and by the early 1900s they developed a bottling facility. Edward became involved in local politics, being a magistrate and vice president of the Manchester Brewers' Association, and from 1907 to 1909 was Lord Mayor of the City of Manchester. On Edward's death in 1928, he had built the company to include eighty-four public houses and thirty-five off-licences. His son, also named Edward, took over and was chairman for over forty years.

In 1951 Joseph Holt Ltd became a public company and in 1968 the second Edward Holt died. Peter Kershaw became chairman and to date this role has

Holt's Brewery, which still remains in the family to this day. (© Ben Abel)

remained within the Holt family. In 1978 the brewery was increased in size and modernised to cope with demand for its beer. Into the 2000s the brewery has gone from strength to strength, offering award-winning beer, and still owns many public houses in the Greater Manchester region.

20. Charter Street Ragged School

Charter Street Ragged School is vitally important in showing a different aspect of Manchester life during the nineteenth century. Located in the notoriously poor district of Angel Meadow, the school provided life's essentials to children considered too poor for 'normal' Sunday school attendance. An industrial school had existed on the site from 1847 but by the 1860s had a reputation for attracting thieves and prostitutes, and many who volunteered there were escorted to and from the school by the police. In its early days, ragged school meetings were regularly held in a warehouse in Mayes Street. In 1861 they moved to nearby Nelson Street. Services included the Band of Hope friendly society, a savings bank and the Nelson Street soup kitchen. The building seen today began in 1866. It contained a girls' home, which for a small fee provided a bedroom and access to the facilities to prevent youngsters from falling into a life of vice. In 1892 it was named the Charter Street Ragged School and Working Girls Home and Manchester Medical Mission. It provided vital poor relief such as food, clothing and medical facilities for those most in need. The medical mission is estimated to have helped around 3,000 people every year.

Above: The former Charter Street Ragged School.

Left: The Ragged School and Working Girls Home – a reminder of a past life.

21. HMP Manchester Prison – Strangeways

HMP Manchester Prison is still informally known by its original name – Strangeways – and is a high-security men's prison that houses over 1,200 inmates. It was opened in 1868 following the closure of the region's New Bailey prison. It was designed by noted architect Alfred Waterhouse and includes a ventilation tower that is a distinctive local landmark on Manchester's skyline. The prison is shaped like a star, with branches radiating out and joining at a central core, designed for guards to see cells in all directions. It was a place for execution until the end of capital punishment in 1965, and up until then around 100 inmates faced execution and was one of only a few prisons in the country that had permanent gallows installed. It held both men and women up until 1963 when it incarcerated men only.

Strangeways Prison has held some notable inmates over the years. For example, suffragettes Emily Davison and Christabel Pankhurst spent short periods there due to their actions when campaigning for women's voting rights. Ian Brady spent time there for theft offences prior to the Moors Murders. More recently, the former GP Harold Shipman was initially held at the prison while awaiting trial.

In April 1990 Strangeways Prison gained notoriety for riots that broke out for twenty-five days. The prisoners challenged the authorities over the deteriorating conditions. The population there had increased well beyond the capacity of the prison, whose Victorian architecture and design were for many fewer prisoners, and with basic facilities not appropriate for the twentieth century. Prisoners were often incarcerated in their cells for around twenty-two hours each day and faced the hated 'slopping out' routine in removing effluence. The prison chapel was taken over and disorder quickly spread, with many prisoners holding a rooftop

Strangeways Prison, designed by Alfred Waterhouse. (© Peter McDermott)

The iconic ventilation tower of Strangeways Prison.

protest. During the riots, most of the interior of the prison was destroyed and the prison was rebuilt at a cost of £50 million. The incident led to the Woolf Report, which provided a blueprint for improvements to the prison service. To date this was the longest lasting breakout in prison history.

22. Barton Arcade

Barton Arcade is an ornate Victorian shopping arcade located between St Ann's Square and Deansgate and is the only surviving arcade of its type in the city. Despite its central location, it is rather a hidden gem in Manchester's display of fine architecture. A four-storey construction of cast iron and glass, it was built in 1871, designed by Corbett, Raby & Sawyer and at the time it was erected to represent Manchester as a cosmopolitan city in a bid to shake off its industrial image. The ornate ironwork and glass were produced by the Glasgow company Walter Macfarlane's Saracen Foundry, who were world leaders in this kind of architectural material. The inspiration for the design came from Milan's Galleria Vittorio Emanuele II, built in 1868, and Manchester followed Italy in building an ornate arcade to showcase the city's wealth and status. Barton Arcade was the start of a fashion in Britain to build more of these opulent shopping paradises. For example, in Manchester a further three were constructed, with Victoria Buildings built in 1874, the Exchange Buildings in 1876 and a further arcade in Deansgate in 1899. However, none of these examples survived, making Barton Arcade very special indeed and one of the best surviving examples of its kind anywhere.

It is U-shaped in design and contains two glass domes and its entrance does little to reveal the inside splendour, with its opulent balconies on each of three upper

Above left: Barton Arcade displaying fine ironwork detail throughout. (© John Hartley)

Above right: Barton Arcade from above. (© Noel Hurley Manchester)

tiers. It attracted a largely middle-class shopper, particularly women. A plaque commemorates the first meeting of the Catenian Association (a society of Catholic laymen), which was held at the arcade in 1908. This group was initiated by Louis Casartelli, who was Bishop of Salford at the time. Barton Arcade became a Grade II listed building in 1972 and underwent restoration in 1980, where many of the original shopfronts were sympathetically replaced to retain its former design.

23. The Printworks

Constructed in 1873, the current Printworks was a former 1870s newspaper printing house that produced newspapers such as the *Manchester Evening Chronicle* and northern editions of key national newspapers such as the *Daily Mirror* and *Daily Telegraph* for over a century. Its first proprietor was Edward Hulton, followed by his son Sir Edward Hulton, who expanded the business. Sir Edward retired in 1924 and a business consortium took control. The building had several names during its time as a printing press, including Withy Gove Printing House, Chronicle Buildings, Allied House, and Kemsley House. By the end of the 1920s, it was the largest printing press in Europe and was often referred to as 'the Fleet Street of the North'. It ceased printing in 1985 and was purchased by the media tycoon Robert Maxwell and renamed Maxwell House, but during the early 1990s, following Maxwell's death and the collapse of his media empire, the building became derelict for over a decade.

The building was close to the IRA bombing of 1996, and as part of the overall reconstruction of the affected area, the building was incorporated into the city centre masterplan that redeveloped the area around Corporation Street and the newly formed Exchange Square. Work began on its transformation at a cost of around £110 million and opened in November 2000 with international singer Lionel Richie and former Manchester United manager Sir Alex Ferguson as guests at the opening event. The building has been sympathetically restored both inside and out, where the visitor is still reminded of its printing press heritage, with some of the original features forming part of the architecture. The Printworks also houses a roof garden, which is one of Manchester's best-kept secrets, containing four beehives, an allotment patch, a beetle hotel and hydroponics unit. The Printworks, alongside the Hard Rock Café, raise donations to local charities through purchases of the locally produced honey.

The Chronicle Building during its heyday.

Above: The Printworks today after significant restoration over recent years, preserving much of its industrial heritage. (© Michael Doherty)

Below left: Beneath the lighting and advertisements for twenty-first-century entertainment lies the Victorian splendour of this impressive Manchester building. (© Charles Welch)

Below right: Looking towards the Printworks from Exchange Square.

24. Minshull Street Crown Courts

Originally known as the City Police and Session Courts, this building is currently Minshull Street Crown Courts. Thomas Worthington's design won the competition for its construction and it was erected between 1867 and 1873. This red-brick building with steep roof design was apparently influenced by Worthington's trips to Italy and has striking similarities to sketches he made during his visits, particularly buildings in the Veneto region, in an Italian Gothic design, though the steeped roof is reminiscent of German architecture. Its final cost was in the region of £81,000, and during the six years it took to construct, the project was hit with a builder's strike for over a year. The design included an impressive clock and bell tower and contains four inner courtrooms, which were located to avoid external noise and retain security. The building was Grade II listed in 1974.

Between 1993 and 1996 the site was extended by architect James Stevenson, and the work included glass coverage of the courtyard and the installation of

Below left: Worthington's clock and bell tower. (© Ben Abel)

Below right: One of Manchester's finest examples of Gothic architecture and the entrance to the current Minshull Street Crown Courts. (© Ben Abel)

six further courtrooms, with designs that complement the original architecture. Today, the courthouse witnesses some of the region's most serious crimes.

25. Jewish Museum

The Jewish Museum was the former oldest synagogue in Manchester. The Grade II listed building was constructed in 1874 and was designed by architect Edward Salomons, whose unique combination of Moorish architecture with Victorian influences gives insights into its past as the former Spanish and Portuguese Jewish synagogue. The synagogue was quite modest in size, holding around 300 people. Edward was the son of a cotton merchant and a notable architect of his time, whose other works include Manchester Reform Club and the building that housed the Art Treasures Exhibition of 1857.

Towards the end of the eighteenth century Jewish communities began trading in the region and many settled in the Cheetham Hill area. The synagogue became redundant when the Jewish population of Manchester moved away from the city centre and settled in the growing peripheral suburbs such as Prestwich and Whitefield. The former synagogue was restored as a museum in 1984. It has remained a museum of Jewish communities in Manchester ever since and is the only museum of its kind outside of London. In 2017 the museum secured nearly £3 million funding to expand its premises, planned for completion in 2020.

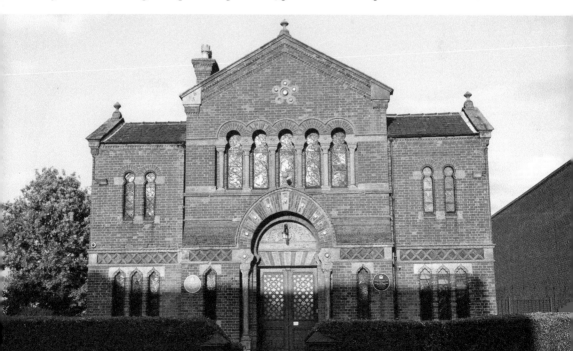

The Jewish Museum, designed by architect Edward Salomons in 1874. (© Ben Abel)

26. Manchester Town Hall

The current Manchester town hall replaced the original building located on King Street, which by the mid-nineteenth century was proving too small for Manchester Corporation's business needs. It also lacked the civic splendour for a city of Manchester's importance. Hence it was decided to build a new town hall that was both functional and filled with civic pride. An architectural competition was won by Alfred Waterhouse's thirteenth-century Gothic triangular design. The Grade I listed building was complete in 1877 after nearly ten years of construction and a cost of almost £1 million. It was officially opened by the mayor of the time, Abel Heywood, who was a champion of the project. One of the twenty-four bells in the clock tower, the great hour bell, is named Great Abel in testament to his support. Waterhouse's work does not disappoint, with its large 280-foot clock tower dominating Albert Square. Above the door are a number of statues including a those of Julius Agricola (to reflect Manchester's Roman origins), Henry III, Elizabeth I and St George. The inscription on the three clock faces, which are visible from Albert Square, depicts, 'Teach us to Number Our Days'. The building was extended in 1938 and overlooks St Peter's Square.

A Victorian postcard of Manchester Town Hall, completed in 1877.

Above: Overlooking Albert Square. (© Ben Ponsford)

Below: Waterhouse's triangular Gothic design dominating Manchester city centre.

The impressive clock tower of the town hall. (© Max Hanna)

The interior reflects both its Victorian origins and Manchester's past. The Sculpture Hall contains statues of notable figures in Manchester's history such as Richard Cobden, John Bright, James Joule, John Dalton and Charles Hallé. The floor contains mosaic tiles of bees and cotton flowers to reflect work and industriousness in the cotton industry. The Great Hall is adorned with the Manchester Murals, depictions of key moments in Manchester's history through twelve paintings by the artist Ford Madox Brown.

It is difficult to imagine that the town hall narrowly escaped demolition during the 1940s when the building was seen as insufficient for modern needs, but thankfully the plans were abandoned. The building is often used for filming since its architecture has similarities to the House of Parliament and is particularly used for shooting political dramas, such as the modern-day film *The Iron Lady*.

27. Manchester Central Convention Centre

The Manchester Central Convention Centre, formerly the G-MEX, is one of England's largest single exhibition halls, and regularly hosts political party conferences, trade and cultural exhibitions. However, its past was very different as the former Manchester Central railway station. Located at the rear of the notable Midland Hotel, the station was opened in 1880. It was designed by Sir John Fowler and modelled on St Pancras station in London where a Manchester to London route was opened and the Midland Hotel was built to mirror the same facilities and architecture at the London end of the journey. It was run by the Cheshire Lines Committee Railway Company (which was an amalgamation of the Great Northern Railway, the Manchester, Sheffield & Lincolnshire Railway and the Midlands Railway) and by the 1870s it was clear that Manchester's London Road station (now Piccadilly) was at full capacity and a further station was required. Its most notable feature is the arched roof, which spans around 64 metres and is one of the largest of its type in the country. It was at its height in the 1930s, catering for over 400 services each day, but it closed in 1969. It remained derelict until the late 1970s when it was purchased by Manchester Council for redevelopment and was remodelled as an exhibition hall and became the G-MEX. Work began in 1982 and, taking around four years to complete, it was officially opened by Elizabeth II in 1986. It was the primary concert venue for Manchester until the opening of the Manchester Arena nearly a decade later. Further restoration took place in 2007 when it changed its name back to its former name of Manchester Central.

Today, Manchester Central is an innovative and creative use of a redundant building. The car park underneath the centre, located in the former goods yard, is unique parking experience, and a historic reminder of the building's former past as the cobbles and rail tracks still sit below the low arches that form the car parking spaces.

Manchester Central station in 1905.

Above: Derelict Central station in 1980.

Below: Manchester Central Convention Centre, formerly the G-MEX. (© Andy Rouse)

G-MEX at night. (© Terry Grealey)

28. Whitworth Art Gallery

The Whitworth Art Gallery dates back to 1887 when Sir Joseph Whitworth left a bequest to develop scholarships and other educational and charitable causes. Whitworth's legacy was managed by Robert Darbishire and the original concept was known as the Whitworth Institute and Park. The institute was managed by a number of Manchester's key public figures including the well-known *Manchester Guardian* proprietor C. P. Scott, local MP William Mather and art dealer William Agnew. The original institute was housed close to the University of Manchester's Owens Building, but it was decided to erect a specially designed space that was completed in 1908.

The gallery was relocated to Whitworth Park on the edge of the University of Manchester's campus (and for which it formally became a part in 1958). The gallery was designed by J. W. Beaumont and intended to attract all classes of people and entice the public away from Manchester city centre and to promote leisure and education. When the University of Manchester took control in 1958 they also refurbished the art gallery in a bid to turn it into 'The Tate of the North'. It was remodelled both in 1995 and 2015, extending the original Edwardian building with modern glass extensions and effectively doubling its size. In 2015 around £15 million was invested in the Whitworth by the University of Manchester and the Heritage Lottery Fund, which dovetailed the gallery with the surrounding parkland.

The Whitworth contains around 55,000 items and focusses on modern art, comprising of artists such as Ford Madox Brown, David Hockney, Vincent van

The Whitworth Art Gallery, designed by J. W. Beaumont and completed in 1908.

Gogh and Picasso. It also specialises in the art of textiles and wallpaper, sculptures and watercolours. It contains an art garden by award-winning designer Sarah Price. In April 2003 the gallery hit the news headlines when three paintings by van Gogh and Gaugin were stolen, though they were later recovered, rolled up but unharmed in some local toilets and were quickly put back on display.

29. Palace Theatre

The Palace Theatre was designed by Alfred Darbyshire and F. B. Smith at a cost of around £40,000, opening in 1891. It was originally the Palace of Varieties and the opening performance was a ballet of Cleopatra. However, during its early days the Palace made little impact on the cultural life of the city and was lucky to survive. The problem was soon identified as the type of performances it offered, which were not especially popular with working-class audiences. The Palace had to broaden its repertoire and popular appeal, and it began offering a more music hall style of entertainment, which improved both ticket sales and the theatre's profits. Here, artists such as Little Tich, Danny Kaye, Gracie Fields, Judy Garland, Noel Coward and Laurel and Hardy took to the stage to a full and vibrant theatre.

Originally the Palace could house around 3,600 people but after renovations in 1913, this was reduced to around 2,600 and currently it can hold just under 2,000 people. During the 1920s and 1930s it became famous for musical productions and pantomime. In September 1940, the theatre took a direct hit from a German bomb during the Second World War air raids of that year, from which it managed to recover. However, by the 1970s, audience numbers declined and once again

The Palace Theatre has survived many threats of closure over the years.

Part of the night-time economy in Manchester, the Palace Theatre continues to thrive to this day. (© Andy Clarke)

the theatre found itself struggling to survive, as did many live venues of the time, and it faced closure in 1979. Once again the Palace was saved, this time through support of the Arts Council and Manchester Council, relaunching its programme of performances, focussing mainly on musical productions. It reopened in 1981 with a new version of *Jesus Christ Superstar*. The stage and other facilities were enlarged and improved to accommodate increasingly large-scale musical productions. Ever since, it has continued to thrive, mainly because of its ability to host major shows, and is one of the few theatres outside London that can do so. The Palace has hosted a variety of touring London musicals, such as *Miss Saigon*, *Les Miserables* and the *Lion King*.

30. The Former Refuge Assurance Building

The former Refuge Assurance Building has provided a distinctive feature on Manchester's skyline for around 130 years. Designed by the notable architect Alfred Waterhouse at the end of the nineteenth century, the former Refuge Assurance Company building is a statement in a Victorian opulent architecture

Designed by Alfred Waterhouse, the former Refuge Assurance Building is one of Manchester's finest architectural features.

of terracotta and includes a dramatic clock tower where each quarter on the dial contains a bee as the symbol of Manchester's former industrial prowess.

The Refuge Friend in Deed Life Assurance and Sick Fund friendly society began business in 1858 by James Proctor and George Robins. It changed its name to the Refuge Assurance Company Ltd in 1881. The company was originally located in Corporation Street, but a new building was planned for construction on a plot of land at the corner of Whitworth Street and Oxford Road. The new Refuge Assurance Building, which took four years to construct, is striking with its terracotta brick exterior and clock tower, and heralded a new type of architecture in the city. Waterhouse moved away from the Gothic style of his other buildings in Manchester, such as the town hall and the University of Manchester's Owens Building. The interior is especially opulent in its décor with marble and glazed brick finish. The building underwent two extensions, first around 1912 by Alfred's son, Paul Waterhouse, and second during the early 1930s by Stanley Birkett. It went from housing around 900 clerks to nearer 1,900 with successive refurbishments. During the Second World War, the building contained two reinforced air shelters for staff and the public and was fortunate not to have suffered any direct hits but incurred minor damage to the roof.

By 1987 the Refuge Assurance Company vacated the premises for a new location in Cheshire. Despite early discussions about it becoming the home for the Hallé Orchestra, these plans never materialised, and the building remained empty until it was refurbished as a hotel and opened in 1996 as the Palace Hotel. The Hallé Orchestra subsequently moved from the former Free Trade Hall into the Bridgewater Hall.

31. The Pankhurst Centre, Nos 60-62 Nelson Street

Located on the edge of Manchester city centre is the former home of suffragette Emmeline Pankhurst and the origins of the Women's Social and Political Union (WSPU). The suffragettes were a group that spearheaded the campaign for voting rights for women. Emmeline and daughter Christabel were prominent figures, leading the movement and partaking in direct action to achieve their aims. The family moved to Nelson Street in 1898 following the death of Emmeline's husband, Richard, and lived there until 1907. The first meeting of the WSPU took place in 1903, and the Pankhurst Parlour has become a physical testament to the suffragette movement.

The suffragettes were active from the turn of the century until the outbreak of the First World War. During this time, their activities became increasingly physical and dangerous and many were imprisoned. Often they would go on hunger strike and faced being force-fed, such was their determination. The Cat & Mouse Act of 1913 was particularly harsh, releasing women very ill from hunger, only to re-arrest them once they were well again. In June 1913 Emily Wilding Davison

The Pankhurst Centre on Nelson Street.

died after falling under the king's horse on Derby Day while campaigning. However, at the outbreak of the First World War they ceased campaigning and put their attention to the war effort. Women over thirty acquired the vote in 1918, and historians have questioned ever since whether it was their pre-war campaigning or their efforts during the war that led to this change of heart by the government. In 1928 women aged over twenty-one were able to vote and it is unfortunate that Emmeline died just before this was implemented.

The building itself dates from around 1840 and was Grade II listed in 1974. Plans to demolish the house were thankfully halted due to campaigns to keep the house and by 1984 the building's restoration began. In 1987 it became the Pankhurst Centre and opened by Emmeline's great-granddaughter, Helen Pankhurst, and MP Barbara Castle. Currently, it is a museum and community centre, which incorporates Manchester Women's Aid, and both organisations work to prevent inequality and domestic abuse.

32. Great Northern Warehouse

This was a former railway goods warehouse that has been transformed into retail outlets, high-quality restaurants, a casino, a sixteen-screen cinema, and other leisure facilities. Built in the late 1890s, it was one of the largest and most advanced centres for the exchange of railway cargo in the country. It was unique

The Great Northern Warehouse. (© Ben Abel)

in its ability to act as a three-way transport centre, where it not only had rail connections but was located close to the Manchester and Salford Junction Canal, which was some 40 feet below ground level. With the canal as an additional means of transportation, and if local roads were included, it encompassed three modes of transport. It had a specialised hydraulic system to move goods from the canal to the ground level and was connected to Manchester's Central station via an iron viaduct.

Its scale is impressive, covering a 9-acre site, and over 267 feet long, five storeys high and dominating Deansgate. Its steel frame and brick construction are apparently fireproof. On each of its four sides, glazed brick depicts its name – Great Northern Railway Company's Goods Warehouse – in an impressive fashion. The canal that ran underneath was closed in 1922 and partially filled in, and the remaining spaces were used as air-raid shelters during the Second World War. By 1954 the warehouse had closed and was left abandoned apart from some car parking facilities. It became a Grade II listed in 1979 but it was not until 1996 that plans were made to turn it into a leisure and retail centre and between 1998 and 2000 the £100 million refurbishment took place. Here, the building retained its Victorian façade yet was carefully restored to reflect both old and new architecture, with a large piazza at its front. More recently the Great Northern has been criticised for not performing to its full potential and plans have come to light to redevelop the building with a further £300 million of investment to revitalise the complex.

33. John Rylands Library

At the end of the nineteenth century one of the finest libraries in the country, if not the world, was created. John Rylands library is an example of Manchester's Victorian and industrial status being showcased to its full potential. The library was founded by Enriqueta Rylands in tribute to her husband John. John died in 1888 and in 1890 Enriqueta found a suitable plot of land and work began on its construction. It opened to the public on New Year's Day 1900. Enriqueta died in 1908.

John Rylands was Manchester's first multimillionaire, having been successful in the family's textile company in St Helens, Rylands & Sons, which he joined in 1819. By 1834 he had moved to Manchester and by the early 1840s was in control of the company. By the mid-1850s he had acquired enough wealth to purchase Longford Hall in Stretford, where he began accumulating a library of books. Enriqueta originally intended to develop a theological library but eventually purchased the 40,000 items of the Althorpe library of the 2nd Earl Spencer, which was the starting point for the library's collections.

The library's neo-Gothic style is attributed to its architect, Basil Champneys, and it is often regarded as his finest piece of work. It took ten years to build at a cost of around £500,000. The main reading room is the focal point for the library, which has a statue of John and Enriqueta at each end and could be mistaken for a church or an Oxbridge college.

John Rylands Library, one of the finest library buildings in the country, opened in 1900. (© Ian Livesey)

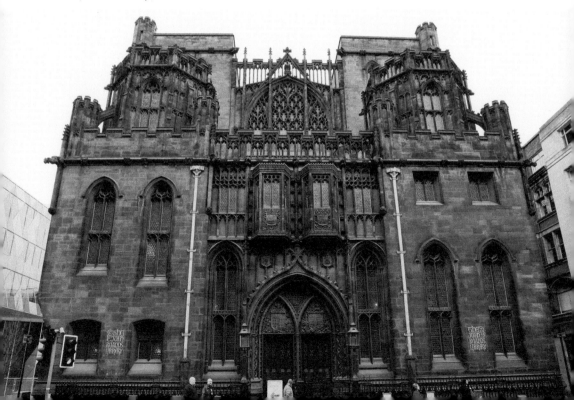

The neo-Gothic style of the building is attributed to its architect, Basil Champneys.

In 1972 the John Rylands Library joined the University of Manchester. In 1994 it achieved Grade I listed status. Between 2003 and 2008 the library underwent major restoration to sympathetically modernise and extend the building. Today, it forms part of one of the largest academic libraries in the UK with over 250,000 books and over a million archival items. These include rare medieval manuscripts, collections by early printer William Caxton, and the personal archives of novelist Elizabeth Gaskell and scientist John Dalton.

34. Midland Hotel

The Midland Hotel is one of the finest hotels ever built in the region. It was opened in 1903 and located next to Manchester's Central railway station. It was built by the Midlands Railway Company to reflect a style of architecture that mirrored the London end of the rail line at St Pancras Hotel and station and the Midland was primarily occupied by transient railway passengers. A covered walkway joined the hotel and train station so that affluent travellers did not suffer Manchester's weather walking between the two buildings. The Grade II listed building was

Left: An early Victorian view of the Midland Hotel, which opened in 1903.

Below: The Midland Hotel in Edwardian terracotta and brick baroque style. (© Tim Green)

The Midland Hotel today. (© Jim McQuade)

designed by Charles Trubshaw in an Edwardian terracotta and brick baroque style. It even included a 1,000-seater theatre that was in operation until 1922. It is believed that in 1904 a meeting between Charles Rolls and Frederick Henry Royce at the hotel led to the formation of the infamous Rolls-Royce Company. Up until around 1910 guests could enjoy a roof terrace, which hosted musical entertainment and great views of the city. However, this closed due to the polluted atmosphere that was not becoming of its high-class visitors. The hotel also incorporated a German restaurant to provide a convivial place for Manchester's German community and it was even decorated with German-style tiles to make the visitors feel welcome.

An urban legend indicates that the hotel was of interest to Adolph Hitler, who had it in mind for Nazi headquarters, had they won the Second World War, and it was allegedly spared from bombing, though this tale has not been proven. Famous guests over the years include Elizabeth II and the Queen Mother, who stayed there as part of their visit to a Royal Variety performance at the Palace Theatre, and the Beatles pop group were refused access to the dining room because they breached the hotel's dress code.

The Midland Hotel remains one of the most iconic buildings in Manchester, hosting a range of important and high-profile events, such as political party conferences where politicians take over the entire hotel, hosting their conferences at the Manchester Central Convention Centre.

Left: Terracotta detail on the Midland Hotel. (© Tony North)

Below: A grand entrance to the Midland Hotel. (© Kie Moon Sung)

35. London Road Fire Station

The ornate architecture of this building disguises its former use as a fire, police and ambulance station and coroner's court. It is a Grade II listed Edwardian baroque design that was constructed in 1906 at a cost of £142,000. It was the headquarters of Manchester's fire brigade until 1974 when a reorganisation resulted in the Greater Manchester Fire Service taking control of local fire services. During its lifetime firemen lived onsite at the fire station in apartments and were on hand to respond to emergencies. Many children grew up at the station and there was a distinct community feel. The fire station was closed in 1986 and remained derelict until the 2010s when redevelopment plans were announced.

The origins of the fire station began at the end of the nineteenth century when a replacement fire station was needed for the one located in Jackson's Row. The site at the corner of London Road and Whitworth Street was identified, but the land was irregular in shape and resulted in an unusual triangular design. A competition was announced for the best design and this was won by John Woodhouse, George Willoughby and John Langham. The use of terracotta was popular at the time and seen in other buildings such as the Refuge Assurance Building and the Midland Hotel, which was mainly used to cope with the city's air pollution. Another design feature was its internal glazed bricks that were also popular. The building housed thirty-eight firemen and had a range of facilities including a laundry, gym and children's play area. In the early days, fire vehicles were horse-drawn and it was not until 1911 that motorised vehicles came into operation. One of its notable

The fire station on London Road, built in 1906.

Fire Station, Manchester

Redevelopment and restoration of this incredible building is awaited.

A reminder of past glories.

design features was its ventilation tower to draw fresh air into the living areas. During the Second World War, it also incorporated an air-raid shelter.

More recently there have been moves to redevelop the declining building. In 2017 proposals to regenerate the site were approved and these plans incorporate a hotel, apartments and other leisure facilities.

36. University of Manchester – Owens Building

The Victoria University of Manchester emerged out of Owens College, which was founded in 1851. Owens College was created through a legacy of £96,942 left in 1846 by the wealthy industrialist John Owens and was originally located on Quay Street. The initial years for the college were difficult since university education was not particularly valued by Manchester merchants, who preferred their sons gain real-time experience by joining family businesses. However, from the 1860s the college created a new vision and its leading professors looked to German universities that emphasised the creation and not just the transmission of knowledge, where research was a key ingredient of university life. It also gave students the experience of facing the unknown and problem-solving. This became

The Owens Building, designed by Alfred Waterhouse in 1873.

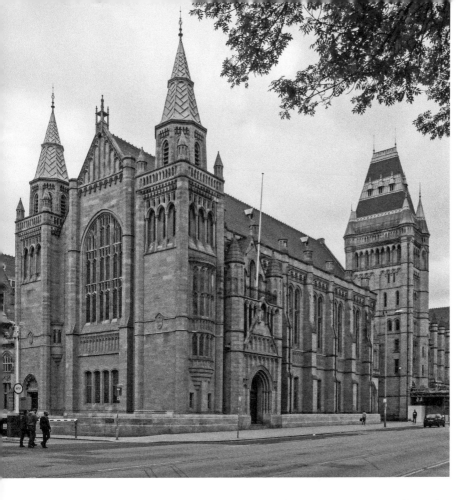

The Owens
Building
today.

a feature of both an education in the humanities as well as the sciences, and a college education finally came to be valued as the key preparation for a professional career.

By 1870 the college required new premises and building began on the current Oxford Road site. The first building, that of the John Owens Building, was completed in 1873. The group of buildings that make up the old quadrangle of the university were finished in 1903 and designed by notable architect Alfred Waterhouse, who had worked on a number of buildings such as Manchester Town Hall, and was known for his neo-Gothic architecture. The new university buildings included the first galleries of the Manchester Museum, whose natural history collection had been amassed by a local society and is one of the best of its kind. From 1873 a large chemistry laboratory on Burlington Street and a new medical school on Coupland Street were constructed. Clinical teaching was provided at the Manchester Royal Infirmary, which remained in Piccadilly until 1908 but later moved to Oxford Road, just south of the university. In 1880 Owens College became the first constituent part of the federal Victoria University.

Today, the University of Manchester is one of the top higher education institutions in the country and part of the Russell Group of top universities. The Owens building remains the focal point for the university.

Designed by Alfred Waterhouse, one of the most famous architects of the era.

37. Old Trafford, Home of Manchester United Football Club

Manchester is famous for its football and Manchester United Football Club's ground at Old Trafford is world renowned. The history of the club dates from 1878 when they were originally known as Newton Heath Lancashire and Yorkshire Railway Football Club. The Football League did not come into existence until 1888 and the Newton Heath Club did not join until 1892. The club moved from Newton Heath to the Old Trafford site in 1910 to a new ground designed by Archibald Leitch with an initial capacity of 80,000. Their first game after its completion was at home to Liverpool FC in February 1910. The Old Trafford ground ceased hosting matches between 1941 and 1949 when the club had to share facilities with rivals Manchester City Football Club's Maine Road ground due to a German bomb essentially destroying the entire ground in 1941. It was reopened in 1949, with a game against Bolton Wanderers. In 1966 the ground was refurbished to allow for the World Cup games when England hosted the event.

MUFC has had some notable managers, including Sir Matt Busby and Sir Alex Ferguson. Sir Alex was probably the most successful, managing the club between 1986 and 2013, making him one of the most prolific managers of his

Old Trafford, the home of Manchester United.

Old Trafford from afar. (© James F. J. Rooney)

generation both in terms of longevity and cup success. The club's domination continued through the 1980s and 1990s, largely under the direction of Ferguson, and he broke former manager Matt Busby's record at the club by 2010. MUFC have had just two of the most successful managers in football in half a century of the club's existence, though since the departure of Sir Alex in 2013, it has struggled to find managerial stability. Currently, Old Trafford has a capacity of almost 75,000, making it one of the largest capacity stadiums in the country. The Sir Alex Ferguson Stand opened in 1996 and is the largest capacity stand of any league ground in England, with over 25,000 seats. In April 2016 the Main (South) Stand was renamed the Sir Bobby Charlton Stand in recognition of the great player and club director.

38. Opera House

Manchester's Opera House opened in December 1912 and was originally known as the New Theatre. It was designed by Farquharson, Richardson and Gill in a classical style with stuccoed bricks and Ionic columns and seats just under 2,000 people. The façade of the New Theatre featured a bas-relief entitled 'The Dawn of the Heroic Age' and beneath it the inscription, 'The Play Mirrors Life'. It became the New Queen's Theatre in 1915. Between 1916 and 1920, the celebrated English conductor Sir Thomas Beecham performed on several occasions, and in 1920 the theatre was renamed the Opera House in his honour.

It closed in 1979 since, like the Palace Theatre, cultural venues suffered in the economic decline of the 1970s. It became a cinema, then a bingo hall, hardly fitting for a building of its cultural significance. However, it returned to its roots as a theatre, reopening in 1984, and continues to offer a range of entertainment but particularly focussing on musicals, ballet and pantomime, and notable shows have included *West Side Story* and *The Phantom of the Opera*. The front of the Opera House contains a series of commemorative plaques in tribute to artists such as Sir Harry Secombe and Roy Castle.

Manchester Opera House. (© Mark Waugh)

39. Central Library

Manchester Central Library is a marvel of the city's interwar architecture. In May 1930, the Prime Minister of the day, Ramsay MacDonald, laid the foundation stone and on 17 July 1934 the library was officially opened by George V and was at the time the largest library supported by a local authority in the country, and is still the second largest after Birmingham. Costing in the region of £600,000, it contained one of the largest library reading rooms after the British Library in London, accommodating 300 people and housing around 1 million books.

Manchester opened the first public lending library in September 1852 at Campfield, after the passing of the Public Libraries Act of 1850. The library soon outgrew its space and was relocated twice, first to the former town hall in King Street and subsequently a section of the infirmary in Piccadilly in 1912. Plans to build a new library had been in existence for some time but the First World War postponed any hope of taking these further.

An architects' competition for the new library was won by E. Vincent Harris, and the unique circular design included an exhibition hall, theatre, research rooms and lecture rooms. Harris had a liking for Roman designs and the Central Library

The Central Library and its unique circular design. (© Max Hanna)

The library has similarities with Emperor Hadrian's Pantheon in Rome.

Manchester Central Library, now housing the Local Studies and Archives Unit. (© Jamie McIlvenny)

is said to have similarities with Emperor Hadrian's Pantheon in Rome, yet its architecture also reflected that seen in American buildings of the time. Central Library is distinctive not only in its circular design but also its white Portland stone exterior and large portico entrance.

The Grade II listed building underwent major refurbishment between 2010 and 2014, and the Greater Manchester Country Records Office joined forces with the library's Local Studies and Archives Unit. The theatre was removed and relocated to the newly formed cultural organisation, HOME, in 2014, which is Manchester's centre for contemporary theatre, film, art and music. Their archives are extensive and include a collection by novelist Elizabeth Gaskell and a theatre collection from the former Theatre Royal, as well as extensive regional records.

40. Kendal's Department Store

This impressive art deco retail store dominates Deansgate in the heart of Manchester. Built in the late 1930s, the origins of Kendal's can be traced back to 1796 when John Watts opened a drapery. The business quickly grew and by 1832 the main store relocated to different premises in Deansgate. Around

Kendal's Department Store and its art deco frontage.

1836 the store was sold by Watts to three employees and the company became Kendal, Milne and Faulkner. Faulkner died in 1862 and the company became Kendal Milne & Co. and here it began expanding into furniture and upholstery. In 1884 Thomas Kendal retired and the daily operations were managed by John Dewhurst Milne. By the 1890s it had opened several departments and a tearoom, catering for Manchester's wealthier clients. A further store was taken across the road and passageways joined the two buildings. During the 1920s it was briefly managed and named after Harrod's famous London store but due to complaints it reverted to its Kendal Milne name. The current building was completed in 1939 and designed by architect J. S. Beaumont. Its design incorporates striking white Portland limestone. In 1921 a tunnel was opened to access both parts of the department store. There was a major fire at the store in 1939 and the tunnel was damaged due to flooding from the water used to extinguish the blaze, which was eventually closed off permanently in 1981 when one of the stores was sold off.

Kendal's was taken over by the House of Fraser group in 1959, though it retained its name until 2005 when it technically became House of Fraser Manchester, but locally it is still known as Kendal's. In 2018 the House of Fraser group was taken over by Mike Ashley of the Sports Direct Group and consequently the store faced an uncertain future but was saved from closure at the end of 2018. Kendal's store is one of the biggest in Manchester, both in terms of size and also with respect to the retailing heritage of the city.

41. CIS Building

The CIS building is the former home of the Co-operative Banking Group. An impressive twenty-eight-storey building, it was constructed in 1962 and at the time was the tallest building in Manchester and for a year after its opening the tallest in the United Kingdom. The Grade II listed building was designed by Gordon Tait and was a showpiece to the co-operative movement that had found its administrative home in central Manchester, originally at No. 1 Balloon Street. It was also designed to modernise Manchester centre and to provide high-quality workspace for its staff. It was awarded a RIBA bronze medal in 1962.

The history of the co-operative movement dates from 1844, where the Rochdale Pioneers developed a system where profits were shared among its members, affectionately known as the 'divi', and the organisation provided cheap goods for those in need, in particular basic foodstuffs.

The Co-op split into different departments, with the Co-operative Wholesale or CWS in 1863 and the Co-operative Insurance Company in 1867. In 1863 the Co-operative Wholesale and Industrial Provident Society Ltd were created in Manchester by local co-operatives in the Lancashire and Yorkshire areas. By 1872 this had grown rapidly, servicing Co-op stores across the country. By 1900 there

Construction of the CIS Building in 1962. The workmen look to be on their lunchbreak.

were almost 1,500 co-operative societies registered around the country and 2 million members. The area around Balloon Street and Dantzig Street has become a famous address for the society's headquarters address and the centre of the wholesale part of the business.

The modern appearance of the CIS building, which used steel, aluminium and glass materials in the construction, was designed to cope with the polluted atmosphere of Manchester in a bid to retain a cleaner appearance and it was also one of the first buildings of its kind to include air conditioning. In 2017 the CIS building was sold for £66 million as the Co-op relocated to their new premises across the road at No. 1 Angel Square. Both buildings have formed part of the NOMA regeneration project around the former Angel Meadow part of the city centre.

The CIS building as the Co-op, relocated to their new premises across the road at No. 1 Angel Square, seen behind the tower.

42. Arndale Centre

Manchester is a Mecca for retail therapy and at its heart is its modern and spacious Arndale Centre, which is one of the largest shopping centres in Europe. It was designed to be the largest undercover shopping centre in Europe when construction began in 1972. Phase one was completed in 1975 and it was finished in 1979. It cost in the region of £100 million and was originally located on a large 15-acre site with a bus station on Cannon Street, parking, offices, and even some domestic flats. When the Arndale opened, it contained over 200 shops and a further 200 market stall holders in its indoor market.

Its concept was in line with other major British cities of the time and began as a great move for the city's redevelopment and modernisation. However, it did have its drawbacks since many old streets and buildings were demolished and the resulting shopping centre was certainly no architectural marvel. Some described it as a giant box full of shops and the yellow tiled exterior made it the butt of jokes. 'The largest public lavatory in the world' was one favourite. Even today there are glimpses of the yellow tiles on the Arndale tower, which reminds us of its 1970s architectural origins that many old buildings suffered demolition for. However, at the time it was seen that Manchester needed a new modern look, economic redevelopment, and a desire to move away from its Victorian past.

The Arndale Tower. (© Tom Blackwell)

Right: The redeveloped Arndale Centre.
(© Tom Blackwell)

Below: The walkway between Marks &
Spencer and the Arndale, which had taken
the full impact of the IRA bomb explosion,
was replaced with a new glass footbridge.
(© Derek Stuart-Cole)

In 1996 the Arndale was devastated by the IRA bombing that exploded right at the heart of the shopping district. The devastation led to plans to redevelop the area and the Arndale was transformed into a light and airy glass construction. Cannon Street and its bus station were removed. The famous walkway between Marks & Spencer and the Arndale that had taken the full impact of the explosion was replaced with a new glass footbridge. Finally, the ugly exterior has largely vanished and Manchester has finally acquired a worthy shopping mall both inside and out.

43. Manchester Arena

Manchester Arena, a modern purpose-built concert venue, opened in 1995 and holds around 21,000 people. It was constructed in preparation for the bid for the 2000 Olympics and funded by the government and the European Regional Development Fund. However, despite the Olympics bid proving unsuccessful, the investment was not in vain since the arena became part of the successful 2002 Commonwealth Games bid. It continues to hold major sporting activities such as boxing matches, basketball and ice hockey. It is home to three major sports teams, the Manchester Storm and Manchester Phoenix Ice Hockey teams and Manchester Giants basketball. Boxing matches have included appearances by the likes of Amir Khan, Mike Tyson and David Haye. It was also in 2002 that it was classed as International Venue of the Year, and Europe's Favourite Arena of the Year in 2008. Since its opening, it has attracted many of the world's artists, such as Pavarotti, Kylie Minogue, Lionel Richie, AC/DC, Cher and local band

The mountain of steps approaching the arena used by thousands who have enjoyed concerts and events here.

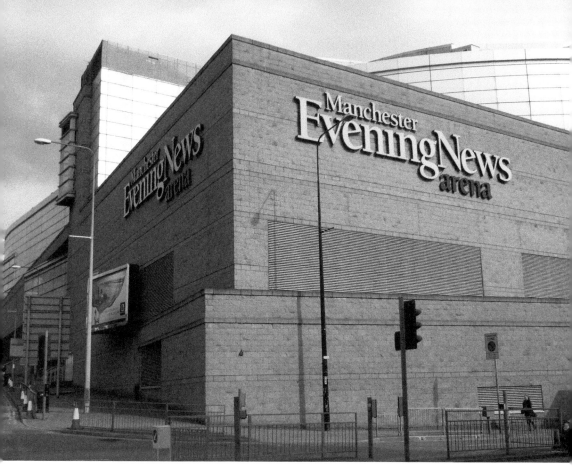

Previously the Manchester Evening News Arena, it is now simply Manchester Arena.

Simply Red, to name just a few. Local comedian Peter Kay is also a regular at the arena, and on one occasion in 2010 he appeared on a record-breaking twenty consecutive nights.

Tragedy struck the arena on 22 May 2017 when it was hit by a terrorist attack and the bomb that was detonated at the end of the Ariana Grande concert killed twenty-two people and injured several hundred. It is difficult to describe both the event and days following, with a strange mix of silence and outpouring of grief. There was a new level of dignity shown by the people of Manchester as the city tried to come to terms with what had happened. The arena was closed until September 2017 and reopened with a benefit concert headlined by local Noel Gallagher, whose signature song 'Don't Look Back in Anger' caught the imagination and spirit of the unfolding events.

44. Bridgewater Hall

Manchester is home to one of the best international concert halls in the world. Opening in 1996, the Bridgewater Hall replaced the Free Trade Hall as the home of the Hallé Orchestra and venue for classical music events. Designed by Renton

Howard Wood Levin Architects, it was a collaboratively funded venture, whose partners included the Central Manchester Development Corporation, Manchester Council and the European Regional Development Fund. The Bridgewater Hall hosted its first event in September of 1996 and was officially opened by Elizabeth II in December of the same year. It also became the home for the BBC Philharmonic and the Camerata.

The Hallé Orchestra originated in 1858 under the auspices of Sir Charles Hallé. He died suddenly in 1895 but his musical legacy continued in his name and over the years the orchestra employed some notable musical talent, like Henry Simon, Gustav Behrens and James Forsyth. One of its most famous conductors was that of Sir John Barbirolli, whose bronze statue can be seen outside the entrance to the Bridgewater Hall. The Hallé survived the Second World War due to Barbirolli's determination and despite some of the musicians being called up for armed service. He conducted concerts in different venues across Manchester after the Free Trade Hall was bomb damaged. The Free Trade Hall reopened again in 1951 and the orchestra had a permanent home once more until 1996 when they relocated.

Despite its post-war reconstruction, the Free Trade Hall was on borrowed time. The desire for a better acoustic experience led to plans for a new concert hall. The Bridgwater Hall is highly unusual in its design which provides the best acoustic experience. Its concrete construction is unique in that the building itself 'floats' on huge springs at its foundations, which enhances the acoustics and eliminates noise and vibration. It houses around 2,400 at any one time and has a tiered design

The Bridgewater Hall, which opened in 1996. (© Andy Rouse)

to ensure maximum positioning for the audience around the stage. The building is also noted for its Marcussen organ, the centrepiece of the hall interior, which houses 5,500 pipes.

45. Cross Street Chapel

Cross Street Chapel is currently a modern place of worship and offices, but the site has a long and fascinating past since a Dissenters' chapel was built on the site around 1694 and is Manchester's oldest nonconformist religious place. Its first minister was Henry Newcome, who founded the chapel. He was a former minister at Collegiate Church from 1657 but refused to adopt the prayers books introduced in 1662 and was persecuted for his actions. He died shortly after the opening of the Dissenter's chapel in 1695. It became an alternative place of worship to the Collegiate Church and Lady Ann Bland, who subsequently built St Ann's Church, was a member of the congregation. The original building lasted until 1715 when it was destroyed by a Jacobite rebellion, led by a blacksmith called Thomas Syddall, and the chapel was awarded £1,500 from parliament for reconstruction.

Into the nineteenth century, Cross Street Chapel became a Unitarian place of worship and attracted Manchester's middle class, who found Unitarianism, a form of religious freedom in line with their business philosophy of free trade. Many middle-class public figures of Manchester life at this time attended the chapel, including cotton merchant John Shuttleworth, John Edward Taylor, one-time editor of the *Manchester Guardian*, and the first Mayor of Manchester, Thomas

Cross Street Chapel.

Potter. The husband of novelist Elizabeth Gaskell, William, was a minister there for over fifty years, from 1828 until his death in 1884. It is believed that Richard Cobden gave his first lecture on the abolition of the Corn Laws at the chapel. During the latter part of the nineteenth century many of the middle class moved to suburbs around the outskirts of Manchester and this affected the size of the congregation. There were plans to abandon the chapel, but these were put on hold at the outbreak of the First World War. However, after the war ended Reverend Johnson became the minister and proved successful in turning the chapel's fortunes around. It was destroyed during the Second World War and replaced during the 1950s. A new chapel that incorporated offices was built in the 1990s.

46. Manchester Aquatics Centre

This is one of the largest and best-equipped swimming pools in the country. It was built to serve the 2002 Commonwealth Games that Manchester hosted. Consequently, the facility is home to a number of international swimming competitions and is the main training facility for the British Paralympics team and the British Polo team. Designed by FaulknerBrowns, its unusual design includes a roof that forms the shape of a wave where the top of this allows for high diving boards. It cost around £32 million to build and it contains two 50-metre pools, which can be subdivided into varying sections according to need, making it the world's most flexible swimming facility.

It was opened in October 2000 by Elizabeth II. It is jointly owned by Manchester Council, the University of Manchester and Manchester Metropolitan University. Since the Commonwealth Games in 2002, it has not only hosted big sporting events but has been a successful community facility for both locals and the higher education community and attracts over a million visitors each year. It provided a training base for the Australian swimming team during the 2012 Olympics hosted by London.

The Manchester Aquatics Centre.

47. The Etihad Stadium, Home of Manchester City Football Club

The current Etihad Stadium was originally the City of Manchester Stadium and was built to host the 2002 Commonwealth Games. The stadium is located in the Eastlands area of the city, a locality that during the post-war period had witnessed a severe economic decline. Plans to build a stadium went as far back as 1989 when Manchester submitted a bid to host the Olympic Games, both in 1996 and 2000, but both failed. However, a bid for the 2002 Commonwealth Games was successful. In the interim, attention remained focused on Eastlands as a place where urban regeneration was badly needed. It was a suitable site for a sporting arena, so plans to redevelop the area continued regardless. There were concerns over building a venue that would ultimately become derelict after any major sporting event so its long-term plans included conversion to a football stadium to retain economic stability for the area.

Manchester City Football Club relocated from their original Maine Road ground in 2003 after agreeing to lease the stadium from Manchester Council. In 2011 it became the Etihad Stadium, named after their new sponsor, and additional investment included a football academy. The scale of the stadium ensures that it also offers a venue for international football and other sporting events and is also used for pop concerts, with its capacity of just under 60,000 people. The stadium cost £112 million to build and was designed by architects Arup Sport. It received accolades for its distinctive concept, including a RIBA award in 2004. Its unique roof is tensioned with sweeping cables that are secured to a number of circular structures surrounding the ground, which are not only practical but add

The home of Manchester City Football Club. (© Bill Lowis)

to the design of the stadium. The stadium forms part of Sportcity, a collection of sporting facilities that include the National Squash Centre and the Velodrome Cycling Centre. In 2015 the Etihad was extended to include a third tier to the South Stand, which was an engineering challenge that retained the design and shape of its unique roof.

48. National Football Museum (formerly URBIS)

Currently this building houses the National Football Museum, but was originally known as URBIS, which reflected its former role as a museum of urban life. Designed by Simpson Haugh & Partners, it was opened in 2002 as part of the redevelopment of the Exchange Square following on from the 1996 IRA bombing. Its initial concept as a museum of urban life offering both permanent and temporary exhibition space did not catch the imagination of the public and visitor

The former URBIS, now the National Football Museum. (© Tom Blackwell)

numbers were disappointingly low, and this was even after the entrance fee of £5 was scrapped. It eventually closed in 2010.

Plans to relocate the National Football Museum from Preston surfaced in 2009 since it was running into financial difficulty. The planned relocation to Manchester was not universally welcome but Manchester Council outbid the Preston consortium, and in 2012 the museum moved into the former URBIS building.

Its architecture is striking. The exterior comprises of around 2,200 panes of glass and is six storeys at one end, with lifts and a vernacular-style staircase, allowing you to take in views of the city. A pinnacle on its roof points toward the city centre. Its current collections include memorabilia from the Football Association and FIFA.

49. Beetham Tower

This is one of the tallest buildings in both the region and the country and was the tallest building outside of London when it was first built in 2006. The forty-seven floor, 170-metre-tall building is a mixture of apartments, penthouses

Below left: Beetham Tower, the home of footballers and celebrities in Manchester. (© Tom Blackwell)

Below right: A mixture old and new. (© Tom Blackwell)

and the Hilton Hotel, which at twenty-two floors takes up half of the building. It is also believed to have the highest home in the country, where the designer, Ian Simpson, owns the most expensive penthouse, at an estimated value of £3 million.

Beetham Tower was built at a cost of £150 million and its unique design includes a 4-metre overhang on the twenty-third floor. Here, a cocktail bar has a glass floor to amaze and frighten at the same time. It is one of the slimmest skyscrapers, and the roof contains a section of glass that projects out as a 'glass blade' that stands 10 metres and which acts a lightning conductor. The original plans were reduced from fifty to forty-seven storeys due to concerns over the sway of the building in windy conditions, though despite this it is known for its humming noise, particularly on windy days. As one of Manchester's more desirable postcodes, Beetham Tower has attracted celebrities and footballers alike.

50. No. 1 Angel Square

This is the new headquarters for the Co-operative group and houses around 3,000 employees. It was completed in 2013 and has formed part of a regeneration of the area around the once notorious Angel Meadow part of Manchester in a project called NOMA (an acronym for North Manchester) that has included around £800 million worth of investment. The building itself cost around £105 million.

No. 1 Angel Square, outstanding and award-winning architecture. (© RA Oliver)

The greenest building in the world and one of Manchester's most iconic modern buildings.

The design looks like the stern of a ship, and inside the building contains a full-height atrium that allows for natural light to illuminate the building, and has been consequently praised for its energy efficient and environmental credentials, maximising daylight and solar energy. In fact, it is the first in the country and one of the largest buildings in Europe to have achieved outstanding BREEAM (Building Research Establishment Environmental Assessment Method) accreditation for sustainability and has been declared the greenest building in the world. It has also won several construction awards including a gold award from the Considerate Constructors Scheme. It was opened by Elizabeth II in 2013. The Co-op moved from the nearby CIS building and it has consolidated a relationship with the Co-operative group that spans back to the nineteenth century with much of its heritage in Manchester.

Bibliography

Books

Harland, J., *Collectanea Relating to Manchester and its Neighbourhood, vol. 1* (Chetham Society, 1866).

Hartwell, C., *Manchester* (Yale University Press, 2001).

Kidd, A., *Manchester* (Edinburgh University Press, 2002).

Parkinson-Bailey, J., *Manchester: An Architectural History* (Manchester University Press, 2000).

Richardson, N., *A History of Joseph Holt* (Swinton, 1984).

Swindells, T., *Manchester Streets and Manchester Men* (5 vols) (J. E. Cornish, 1906–08).

Woodman, D., *The Story of Manchester* (History Press, 2017).

Websites

www.barbirollisociety.co.uk
www.Coop.co.uk
www.gaskellsociety.co.uk
www.hiddengem.catholicfaith.co.uk/history
www.houseoffraserarchive.co.uk
www.joseph-holt.com
www.manchester.ac.uk
www.manchestercathedral.org
www.manchestereveningnews.co.uk
www.mancity.com
www.manutd.com
www.palacetheatremanchester.net
www.stannsmanchester.com

Manchester, a city of contrasting architecture and culture.

Acknowledgements

Paul Rabbitts would like to thank all the photographers who have donated images free of cost and who have highlighted the wonderful buildings of Manchester. I would especially like to thank Deborah, whose work much of this book is based on. An absolute pleasure to work with.

Deborah Woodman would like to thank the people of Manchester both past and present who have made Manchester the great city it is. Deborah would also like to thank Paul for his boundless enthusiasm and commitment to this project.

About the Authors

Paul Rabbitts is a landscape architect and Head of Parks at Watford Borough Council and is the author of fifteen books, ranging from the history of Cassiobury Park in Watford to the iconic Victorian bandstand, and has also written several books on architecture.

Dr Deborah Woodman is a Research Development Officer at the University of Salford. Her research is focused around the history of north-west England, the role of drink in society, commerce and trade, and popular politics of the nineteenth century. She has taught history at the universities of Huddersfield, Salford and Manchester Metropolitan University.